MW00876937

# My Catholic Faith Picture Book A-Z

## Marti Genge

*Lord God Almighty, I thank you for all the blessings you have given me.*
*Thank you for the life full of happiness and love.*
*You have provided me with everything I need.*
*You gave me my family and friends, who inspire,*
*encourage, and bless me with love and kind words.*
*They are always there to lift me up when I feel down and in sorrow.*
*If not because of you, I won't be loved this much.*
*Thank you, oh lord, for your glorious and unwavering love and kindness.*
*Even with my sins and misgivings that made you suffer in the Cavalry,*
*you still give me the people who you knew can love and protect me*
*the way you want to love and protect me as my Father.*
*Lord, may all the families that grace these pages, find your love and happiness.*
*For along with the Mother of God Mary Most Holy,*
*give them the nourishment that only you can give. Amen*

ISBN– 13:978-1490410210
ISBN– 10:149041021X

Visit this website for more information:       www.parentingbeyondthepew.com

Altar

Altar Server

 Angel

# Bb

Bells

Bible

Bishop

Blessing

# Cc

Chalice

Church

Crucifix

Holy Communion

# Dd

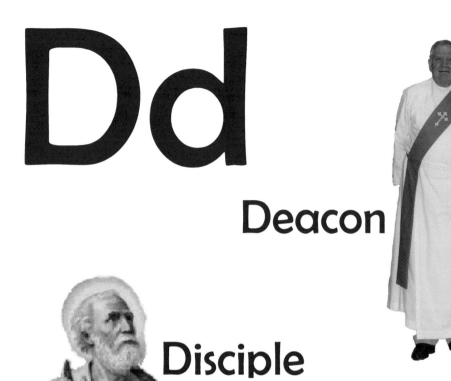

Deacon

Disciple

Door

# Ee

Easter
Candle

Eucharist

# Ff
Holy Family

Font
Holy
Water

Font
Baptismal

First
Communion

# Gg

**Genuflect**

**God**

**Grace**

**Guardian Angel**

# Hh Hands Praying

## Holy Spirit

## Host

# Ii

Incense

Infant Jesus

✝✝✝✝✝✝✝✝✝✝✝✝✝✝✝✝✝✝✝✝✝✝✝✝✝✝✝✝✝✝

# Jj

## Jesus Christ

## St. Joseph

# Kk

## Kneel

## Kneeler

# Ll

## Last Supper

## Lectern

## Lord's Prayer

Our Father, Who art in Heaven,

Hallowed be Thy Name;

Thy kingdom come,

Thy will be done,

on earth as it is in Heaven.

Give us this day our daily bread;

and forgive us our trespasses,

as we forgive those

who trespass against us;

and lead us not into temptation,

but deliver us from evil.

Amen

# Mm

Mary

Monstrance

# Nn

Nighttime prayer

Nun

# Offertory basket

# Holy Oils

# Organ

# Pp

Pope

Priest

# Qq

Quiet

# Rr

Relics

Rosary

Reconciliation

# Ss

Saint Therese

Sign of the Cross

Singing

# Tt

## Tabernacle

## Ten Commandments

**TEN COMMANDMENTS**

I AM THE LORD YOUR GOD. YOU SHALL NOT HAVE STRANGE GODS BEFORE ME.

II YOU SHALL NOT TAKE THE NAME OF THE LORD YOUR GOD IN VAIN.

III KEEP HOLY THE SABBATH.

IV HONOR YOUR FATHER AND YOUR MOTHER.

V YOU SHALL NOT KILL.

VI YOU SHALL NOT COMMIT ADULTERY.

VII YOU SHALL NOT STEAL.

VIII YOU SHALL NOT BEAR FALSE WITNESS AGAINST YOUR NEIGHBOR.

IX YOU SHALL NOT COVET YOUR NEIGHBOR'S SPOUSE.

X YOU SHALL NOT COVET YOUR NEIGHBOR'S GOODS.

## Trinity

# Uu

TEN COMMANDMENTS

I AM THE LORD YOUR GOD. YOU SHALL NOT HAVE STRANGE GODS BEFORE ME.

II YOU SHALL NOT TAKE THE NAME OF THE LORD YOUR GOD IN VAIN.

III KEEP HOLY THE SABBATH.

IV HONOR YOUR FATHER AND YOUR MOTHER.

V YOU SHALL NOT KILL.

VI YOU SHALL NOT COMMIT ADULTERY.

VII YOU SHALL NOT STEAL.

VIII YOU SHALL NOT BEAR FALSE WITNESS AGAINST YOUR NEIGHBOR.

Unity

Vatican

Vestments

Holy Water

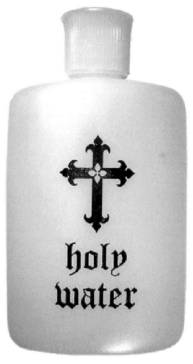

holy water

Way
Of
The
Cross

# Xx

Saint
Francis
Xavier

# Yy

**YOU**
in the
pew
with
family

# Zz

zzzz sleeping, coZy,
amaZing lovable you!

# Activities For Parents

This fun and interactive book will be a keepsake for many years. Here are some more ideas to inspire, educate and explore the pages of this book. In general picking out colors from the borders, pointing out the alphabet, and counting the number of images on the page are ways to use this book. Relate to the images with stories about when you were a little child. Below are more ideas for each letter.

A: Point out all the items on the altar. Explain about Angels. Name an altar server that you know.

B: Discuss the sound of the bells. Talk about the many blessings you receive at church. Tell your child your Bishop's name.

C: Tell an imaginary story about walking into the church and point out all the images in the church. Point out the Crucifix on the page and in the photo of the church.

D: What does the door at your church look like? The Disciple is St. Peter, whom Jesus had chosen.

E: During Mass point out the Eucharist as the Priest raises it.

F: Show where your fonts are.

G: Teach your child the Guardian Angel prayer

H: Put their hands in yours as they point up in prayer.

I: Explain that incense is prayers going up to heaven.

J: Show the difference from various pages of Jesus as an infant, baby and adult.

K: Point out how the little boys hands are together as he prays.

L: Count how many are at the Last Supper.

M: Monstrance is a big word, but just the sound will help them become familiar. Teach them the Hail Mary.

N: Start at the infant stage of your child in saying a nighttime prayer.

O: Sing a song that the organ might play.

P: What is your priest's name and also the Pope's?

Q: How are we in church? For toddlers, talk about this at home before you go to church. Set your expectations and consequences then.

R: Buy a rosary for little children. Let them get use to the feel.

S: Practice the Sign of the Cross. You can start that early.

T: Just talking about the images will help them as they grow older.

U: Pick out an image from page and try to find it somewhere else in the book.

V: What color is the priest wearing today?

W: Get a container and bring Holy Water home. Start a tradition of blessing each other at a time you as a family choose.

X: Explain how St Xavier loved Jesus like you do.

Y: Count how many in your family will fit in the pew. Who will sit behind you or in front of you?

Z: Sometimes for little ones it's hard to stay awake during mass. Let them know that God loves them!

CPSIA information can be obtained
at www.ICGtesting.com
Printed in the USA
LVIC04n1600190716
496924LV00014B/103